Painting Shorebird Decoys

16 Full-Color Plates and Complete Instructions

by Anthony Hillman

DOVER PUBLICATIONS, INC., NEW YORK

To the memory of
Joseph P. Hillman

Published in Canada by General Publishing Company, Ltd., 30 Lesmill Road, Don Mills, Toronto, Ontario.
Published in the United Kingdom by Constable and Company, Ltd.

Painting Shorebird Decoys: 16 Full-Color Plates and Complete Instructions is a new work, first published by Dover Publications, Inc., in 1987.

Manufactured in the United States of America
Dover Publications, Inc., 31 East 2nd Street, Mineola, N.Y. 11501.

Library of Congress Cataloging-in-Publication Data

Hillman, Anthony.
  Painting shorebird decoys.

  1. Decoys (Hunting)—Painting. I. Title.
TT199.75.H55 1987   745.593   86-32799
ISBN 0-486-25349-X

Painting Shorebird Decoys

After you have carved a shorebird decoy, or purchased an unfinished carving, you will want to color it faithfully according to species. Prior to 1918, when plover, snipe and curlew were legal game, most of the old shorebird decoys were painted in a stylized manner, varying from the extremely crude to the unique and beautiful. My purpose in creating this book has been to provide instructions and helpful tips to modern-day painters of shorebird carvings, no matter what their preferred style of painting may be. I have included sixteen full-color plates of profile and top-view illustrations as a source of accurate information on shorebird coloration. As of this writing, no publication has yet provided full-color top-view reference illustrations of shorebirds. The plates in this book show sixteen species of adult birds in their spring plumage. This is breeding plumage, when these birds are at their brightest and most colorful. By contrast, in fall and winter most species are a dull gray or brown above and white below. In all of the birds illustrated, the males and females are similarly plumaged.

Although these plates are the best painting guide available in book form and should be studied closely, the beginner cannot expect to be able to duplicate complex shorebird coloration without some practice. Seldom can the exact color desired be squeezed right from a tube of paint. Many colors can be created only by the blending of pigments—and don't be afraid to experiment—but even basic colors vary depending on the type of paint (acrylics, oils, etc.) and the manufacturer.

Don't let this intimidate you. Study the instructions, plates and other sources carefully, and practice mixing and applying paints, but also do not be afraid to draw upon your own creativity. Discovering your own "recipes" is part of the fun of decoy painting. There is no one way to paint a decoy. Gradually you will develop a personal style that you will be proud of.

RESEARCH YOUR SUBJECT

Before you begin painting, it is essential to study your subject carefully. Learn the different topographical features of a shorebird (see Figure 1). This will help you remember where to apply the proper colors and markings. Feather shape and size often determine the color pattern, and therefore determine how you apply paint to your decoy.

Study the color illustrations on Plates 1 through 16. These plates, which include both profiles and top views, may be removed from the book so that the appropriate one can be placed beside your carving and referred to as you paint. Supplement the plates with color photographs and, wherever possible, live or preserved specimens. Thorough research is important; study skins are invaluable but sometimes difficult to obtain. If you are studying preserved specimens, double-check against the illustrations for the proper coloration of the bill and any fleshy parts represented in your carving, as the colors of live birds fade after death. Learn to identify the true coloring of your subject. This point is especially important in depicting shorebirds, as it is not unusual to see a complete spectrum of plumage phases on individuals within a single flock. As migrating birds return from their northern breeding grounds in the fall, some will still be in breeding plumage, while others may already be replacing this with their winter feathers in varying degrees. Add the fact that the plumage of juvenile birds differs somewhat from both summer and winter plumage of the adult birds, and you can see why careful observation is important. Making such observations can be one of the most enjoyable parts of painting bird carvings.

BRUSHES AND PAINTS

When choosing any art supplies, a good rule to follow is to buy the best, or at least the best you can afford. This rule applies especially to brushes, since the brush is the instrument that gets the paint onto the surface of your carving. A wide variety of brushes is available for any paint medium you use. Figure 2 illustrates some types of brushes I find useful for painting decoys. If brushes of the type you desire are not available locally, write for catalogs from some of the major art-supply firms. It will be futile to attempt to paint with inferior brushes.

Through the years I have become partial to sign-

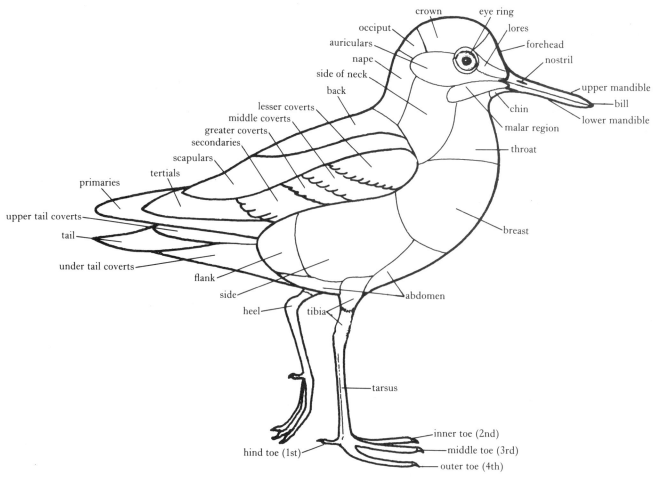

Fig. 1. TOPOGRAPHY OF A SHOREBIRD (*Red Knot*)

painting and lettering brushes. The longer bristles on these brushes hold more paint and make it easier to control long, delicate lines. They also help keep paint from getting up into the ferrule, an important advantage when working with acrylics (for which your brush also should have a soft, white, nylon type of bristle).

The "fan blender" is another useful brush, both for blending colors and for "dry-brush" technique. With this type of brush, I prefer white oil bristles, even for acrylic paints, as the stiffer bristles maintain the proper fan shape.

For applying large, solid areas of color, the larger-size "flats" (brushes with flattened ferrules) are the most useful. These brushes deliver a large quantity of paint while allowing good control where sharp edges are desirable.

In time you will find that some of your brushes are losing their shapes, their hairs twisting in every direction. Save these worn-out tools. Although they may no longer serve the specialized purposes you purchased them for, they can be invaluable for stippling and dry brushing.

Just as different kinds of brushes serve different purposes, different types of paint have different properties and produce different effects. Oil paints have the major disadvantage of taking a long time to dry. This can also be an advantage, however, as it permits colors to be blended to perfection. And if you make a mistake, the area can be wiped clean to start over again. If drying time is of no concern, you may prefer oils, for they produce a rich, almost sensual, gloss that seems to be obtainable with no other medium.

The two basic media for oil paint are turpentine and linseed oil. Turpentine will reduce drying time and deaden the sheen inherent in tube colors. Linseed oil, when added to paint, extends drying time and adds sheen. Several drying agents, such as cobalt drier, are available. Allowing oil paints to stand overnight on absorbent brown paper (like that used to make shopping bags) will drain off some of the linseed oil, as is preferred by some decoy carvers.

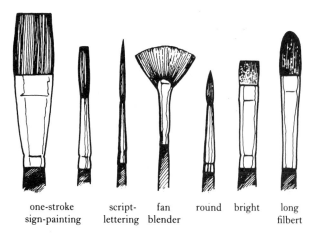

| one-stroke sign-painting | script-lettering | fan blender | round | bright | long filbert |

Fig. 2. TYPES OF BRUSHES

(Instructions continue after plates.)

Plate 1. Sanderling

Plate 2.   Killdeer

Plate 3. Common Snipe

Plate 4. American Oystercatcher

Plate 5. Red Knot

Plate 6. Greater Yellowlegs

Plate 7.   Ruddy Turnstone

Plate 8. Black-bellied Plover

Plate 9. American Avocet

Plate 10. Long-billed Curlew

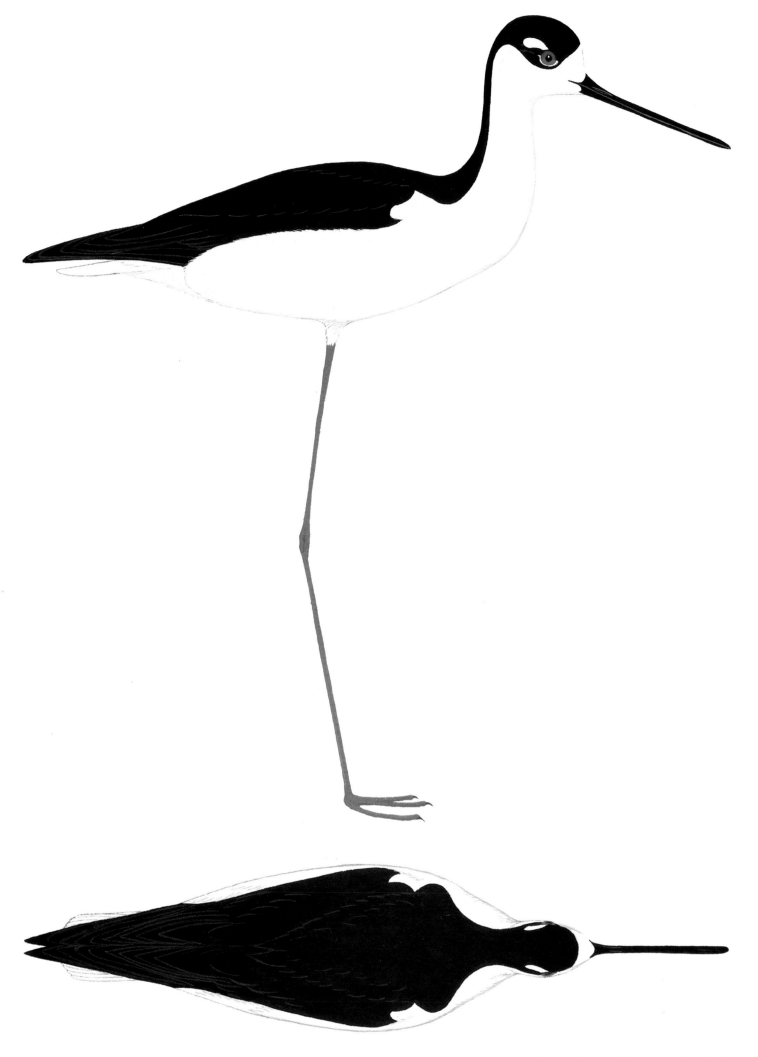

Plate 11. Black-necked Stilt

Plate 12. Dunlin

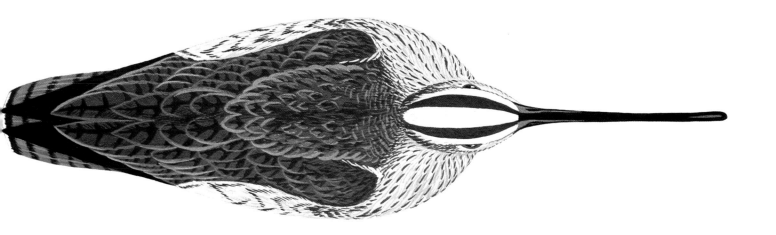

Plate 13.   Whimbrel

Plate 14. Piping Plover

Plate 15. Spotted Sandpiper

Plate 16. Short-billed Dowitcher

Acrylic paint is probably the medium most widely used by carvers of decoys. It dries quickly, and brushes can be cleaned in soap and water, making acrylics more convenient than oils for most people. *It is important to remember that for acrylic paints you must use acrylic primer.*

The speed at which acrylic paints dry can be a handicap for the beginner, but practice and familiarization with the medium soon overcome this difficulty. A gel medium, available in art-supply stores, slows drying time when added to tube acrylic paints.

Tube acrylics tend to dry with a slick surface. Given the requirements of decoy painting, this is not necessarily desirable. I use flat exterior house paints as the main colors of my palette. Flat acrylics offer a distinct advantage when you are painting undercoats and thin washes of color, there being less chance of running or puddles of pigment remaining when the brush is lifted off the painting surface. Another advantage is that when additional markings are applied, as in feathering, the flat finish takes the applied color better.

Usually house paints are sold in quart cans. You may find it awkward to work from these directly, but transferring enough paint for several projects to smaller containers works fine. Basic colors available in flat house paints include black and white (from which you can also make gray) and brown. You may use tube colors and tints to achieve reds, blues, yellows and other colors. This combination of house and tube paints is my personal preference. In any case, remember that it is easier to make the flat finish of a completed piece glossy (if you desire it) than to tone down a glossy finish to a soft luster.

SELECTING YOUR COLORS

If you have never painted a shorebird, start with a species that possesses a relatively simple pattern. As you look through the plates in this book, you will find that the oystercatcher (Plate 4), black-necked stilt (Plate 11), plovers (including the killdeer; Plates 2, 8 and 14) and avocet (Plate 9) have simpler, bolder patterns than the other birds. An oystercatcher can teach the novice painter much about the mixing of colors and their application to a three-dimensional object. On the other hand, since the sanderling is the best-known American shorebird, I have thought it advisable to include the most detailed instructions, below, for painting this somewhat more complexly marked species. If you wish to begin with the simpler oystercatcher, I have also provided the procedures for that bird. Read through the sanderling instructions first, however.

The exact colors you use will of course be determined by the particular species represented by your carving. After the instructions for painting the sanderling and the oystercatcher, I have provided a list of specific colors you will need for painting the fourteen other birds. Remember that you will have to create many of these colors by mixing. The following basic colors, however, are needed for all or at least most of the species illustrated:

1. White.
2. Black.
3. Burnt umber. (With flat house paints you must check color samples, as each manufacturer may market several brown shades under different trade names. An example is Cook & Dunn's "Cape Cod Brown," an excellent dark brown once a small amount of black has been added.)
4. Burnt sienna.
5. Raw sienna.
6. Indian red.

With the addition of a medium gray (which you may create, of course, by mixing black and white), these colors will provide the painter with the bulk of what he needs. Other colors necessary in smaller quantities include:

7. Ultramarine blue.
8. Cadmium yellow, medium.
9. Hooker's or deep green. (For the legs of certain species, usually mixed with raw sienna.)
10. Red. (Note: Most tube colors that look like "fire-engine red" are sold under such trade names as "Grumbacher red," "Winsor red," etc. Be sure to check color samples before purchasing.)
11. Cadmium orange.

Besides actual paints, a wide variety of colors is available in tints. The Rich Lux Products Company of Philadelphia puts out an excellent line known as "Minit Tint." The beauty of tints is that, since they contain no hardeners or driers, they have an extremely long shelf life under moderate temperature conditions. Be sure to follow instructions to determine the maximum amount of tint that can be safely used. Applying too much will prevent proper drying.

BEFORE YOU BEGIN

After you have sanded your carving to a smooth finish, it is necessary to seal the wood. Clear wood sealers include lacquer and shellac. Two coats are usually sufficient. Sand between coats with #220 or finer sandpaper. Wood that contains knots needs to be carefully sealed, as the resins in knots will discolor paint.

Once it has been sealed, your carving should be primed. Priming further protects the wood and provides a uniformly pigmented surface to paint on. Remember to use oil-based primer when you are painting with oils, acrylic primer when you are using acrylic paints. When you paint with acrylics, you may want to start with an oil primer and then coat this with acrylic primer. Acrylic primer applied directly to the wood raises the grain, an effect you may prefer. This requires more sanding, but it allows the natural beauty of the grain to show through.

"Kilz," made by Masterchem Industries, is an excellent product that I recommend. Since this is a primer-sealer, it allows you to prime and seal in one operation, saving you a step. Best of all, it can be covered with either oils or acrylics. When using acrylics, however, it is a good idea to top it with a coat of an acrylic primer.

While brushing on any coat of primer, be sure not to leave ridges or brush marks, the presence of which will make painting of details more difficult later on. After the primer has dried, sand a final time with #220 or finer sandpaper. This will remove any roughness, providing a smooth base to paint over.

NOTE: Read and follow the instructions found on the labels of all primers, sealers and paints you may use. Familiarize yourself with the qualities of each product as well as precautions necessary for their safe use.

PAINTING A SHOREBIRD DECOY—STEP BY STEP

Now you are ready to paint your shorebird carving. The following detailed procedures for painting a sanderling (in spring plumage) will give you a good idea of how to go about painting any shorebird. You may want to begin with the oystercatcher, however, a simpler painting project than the sanderling. In that case, first read through the instructions for the sanderling, then follow the specific instructions I have added for the oystercatcher.

To paint the sanderling (refer to Plate 1), start by marking the areas of color with a pencil (an ordinary #2 lead pencil is fine) to define their boundaries. At this early stage, the carving should be all white, as that is the color of most primers (if your primer is not white, you will need to top it with a coat of white paint). Now mix a reddish brown (as always, determine the precise shade by referring to the plate and your other sources) by adding a slight amount of raw sienna to a base of burnt sienna; apply this solid color to the breast, head and neck.

Next, mix black and white to make a light gray for the secondaries and tertials. Refer to the top view and note that the gray becomes almost black as it approaches the wing coverts on the "shoulder" (actually the second joint of the folded wing). You can either gradually mix more black with the gray as you paint from back to front, or mark off the dark area and paint it separately. At this point you should have a gray that shades gradually to near black, as shown in the illustration. Note that we are still dealing only with solid colors and basic color areas. The details will be added later.

The primary wing feathers should be painted next. I usually add a small amount of brown to black as I feel that this dilutes the color strength of black in this area, which should help soften the appearance of these dark wing feathers. Now paint the tail. The tail of the sanderling is a very dark gray (almost black) at the tip but becomes a lighter gray toward its base. At the comple-

tion of this step, the carving should look as follows. The head, neck, breast and back (including the scapulars) should be a solid reddish brown. The tertials, secondaries and wing coverts should be gray, shading from medium gray on the tertials to almost black at the "shoulder." The primaries should be brownish black, and the tail very dark gray at the tip, shading to a lighter gray at the base.

It is a good idea to paint the legs (represented usually by just a single dowel on a decoy-style carving) and the bill last. Paint on surfaces as prominent as these is readily subject to accidental smearing. Should you need to rest or hold the carving in order to steady it while painting the body, you will not mar a painted surface if you save the legs and bill for last.

Now you can lay out individual groups of feathers with a pencil, proceeding afterwards to individual feathers. It is very important to study the top view at this point. Drawing a temporary center line down the bird's back will help you keep things straight as you define the shapes of the feathers on the various parts of the wings and body.

The procedure I am about to describe is suitable, with appropriate modifications, for the detailed feather painting of all shorebird decoys. First check once again that you are satisfied with the base colors and that the border of each section is sharp-edged and accurately located. At this point each major feather should have been defined in pencil. Now, starting from the tail, define the edge of each tail feather in medium gray. Refer to the plate as often as necessary. Next, with a dark gray, similarly edge and define the primary flight feathers. This same dark gray paint can be used to add the markings found within each tertial, secondary and wing covert. After these markings are dry, some highlights of sienna can be added. Finally, edge each feather with a fairly light gray as shown on the plate.

The back, neck, head and breast are now ready to be painted in detail. Referring to the plate, paint black markings on each feather, as shown, starting at the scapulars and proceeding to the smaller feathers toward the nape of the neck. Note the dark markings at the side of the breast. These are colored with a mixture of black and burnt sienna. As you paint toward the neck, add a greater proportion of the burnt sienna to capture the gradual lightening of these feathers. With the medium brown that results, define the dark area of the lores (area between the eye and bill). This dark area continues to run in an arch from the back of the eye to the nape. A dark line of this sort may be found on many sandpipers and other species of shorebirds. Now go back to the side and breast and edge the dark brown markings with a mixture of white and burnt sienna. This same highlighting effect should be used to give the auriculars (the "cheeks") a fuller look. Now use white to edge the scapulars and other back feathers.

Paint the eye and the white eye ring and add some fine white feathering to the area between the base of the bill and the forehead. With a light gray, add the details to the flanks and under tail coverts. Now you can paint the bill and the legs black. If you wish, add details (such as nostrils) in gray or light brown, as shown. If you have followed these instructions and the color plate carefully, you should now be looking at your fully painted carving. Congratulations!

The procedure for painting a boldly marked bird like the American oystercatcher (Plate 4) is basically the same. After studying Plate 4, carefully mark with a pencil the borders of each area of color. I strongly advise you to mark off the outside of the eye ring at this point. That will enable you to avoid painting this area when applying the head color. It will be difficult to give the eye ring its proper bright red coloring if you must paint over black. When you have pencilled in all the color borders, you are ready to begin painting.

Add a small amount of burnt umber to black and use this to paint the tail and wing primaries. Next, using burnt umber mixed with a very small amount of black, coat the tertials, scapulars, wing coverts and back as shown in the illustration. Now, with the same mixture of black and umber used on the tail and primaries, paint the head, the breast and the area just behind the nape as indicated. Remember to be careful as you paint around the eyes and the edge of the bill. Once you have a flat coat of color applied to the major areas you are ready to add some details. First, edge the tail and primaries with a dark brown just light enough to contrast with the almost black paint already laid on these parts. To highlight the "cheeks" and indicate breast feathering use a medium brown on the head and breast as shown. Don't overdo it! Be subtle with your highlights.

Edge the tertials and scapulars with a mix of raw sienna and a small amount of burnt umber. The darker feathering on the brown back and wing feathers is created with burnt umber mixed with just enough black to make it contrast with the underlying brown. The eye ring (which is fleshy on the living bird) and the uniquely shaped bill are colored with red to which a minute amount of cadmium yellow, medium, has been added. Use the cadmium yellow for the iris, and black with a dot of white for the pupil. Finally, paint the legs the proper flesh color. For this, mix white with a small amount of red and add a minute amount of cadmium orange. You will notice that I am not advising you to buy a tube of ready-mixed flesh-colored paint; colors of this nature that you mix yourself are usually superior to the ready-made product. Details on the legs may be added in a darker flesh color. This will complete the oystercatcher.

With practice you will acquire familiarity with the effects of different paints, tools and procedures. Do not strive for speed; it will come on its own. The coloring shown on the plates can be simplified if you prefer to imitate the old "gunning style" shorebird decoy. On the other hand, if you are interested in accuracy of detail, more research will enable you to improve on these color schemes. Good luck!

For your convenience, the colors of the paints needed for the decoys illustrated on Plates 2, 3 and 5 through 16 are given below. Remember, however, that pigments vary from manufacturer to manufacturer and with the type of paint. In many cases you will need to experiment with different mixtures to achieve a particular color. Some of the colors listed may be created by mixing others. And you may work out any number of satisfactory substitutions. The following list is intended only as a rough guide.

LIST OF COLORS

PLATE 2. Killdeer: Black; white; burnt umber; red; burnt sienna; cadmium yellow, medium.

PLATE 3. Common Snipe: Black; white; burnt umber; raw sienna; burnt sienna; Hooker's green.

PLATE 5. Red Knot: Black; white; burnt umber; Indian red; raw sienna; Hooker's green.

PLATE 6. Greater Yellowlegs: Black; white; burnt umber; cadmium yellow, medium.

PLATE 7. Ruddy Turnstone: Black; white; Indian red; red; cadmium orange.

PLATE 8. Black-bellied Plover: Black; white; burnt umber.

PLATE 9. American Avocet: Black; white; cadmium orange; raw sienna; ultramarine blue.

PLATE 10. Long-billed Curlew: Black; white; burnt umber; raw sienna; red.

PLATE 11. Black-necked Stilt: Black; white; red.

PLATE 12. Dunlin: Black; white; Indian red; red.

PLATE 13. Whimbrel: Black; white; burnt umber; ultramarine blue; red.

PLATE 14. Piping Plover: Black; white; cadmium yellow, medium; burnt umber.

PLATE 15. Spotted Sandpiper: Black; white; burnt umber; red; cadmium yellow, medium.

PLATE 16. Short-billed Dowitcher; Black; white; Indian red; raw sienna; burnt umber; Hooker's green.